Published by
North Atlantic Books
P.O. Box 12327
Berkeley, California 94712

Cover art by Katya Korobkina
Cover and book design by David Ruppe
Printed in the United States of America

Green Smoothie Magic is sponsored by the Society for the Study of Native Arts and Sciences, a nonprofit educational corporation whose goals are to develop an educational and cross-cultural perspective linking various scientific, social, and artistic fields; to nurture a holistic view of arts, sciences, humanities, and healing; and to publish and distribute literature on the relationship of mind, body, and nature.

North Atlantic Books' publications are available through most bookstores. For further information, visit our website at www.northatlanticbooks.com or call 800-733-3000.

Library of Congress Cataloging-in-Publication Data

Boutenko, Victoria.

 Green smoothie magic / Victoria Boutenko ; illustrations by Katya Korobkina.

     pages cm

 Summary: "With this story of a boy who learns about the miracles of plant life and the pleasures of drinking blended vegetables and fruits, Victoria Boutenko imparts to young children her enthusiasm for raw foods and healthy eating"— Provided by publisher.

 Audience: 4–11.

 ISBN 978-1-58394-601-5

1. Nutrition—Juvenile literature. 2. Smoothies (Beverages)—Juvenile literature. I. Korobkina, Katya, illustrator. II. Title.

 RA784.B6388 2013

 613.2—dc23

2012050161

Printed and bound by QuaLibre/CGPrinting, June 2013, in the United States. Job #113.

1 2 3 4 5 6 7 8 9 QuaLibre/CGPrinting 18 17 16 15 14 13

Green Smoothie Magic

By Victoria Boutenko

Illustrations by
Katya Korobkina

North Atlantic Books
Berkeley, California

My name is Nic. I am already six.

I live with my mom, dad, and my baby sister Lily.

My daddy is a pilot. He is big and strong. I also want to grow to become big and strong, just like my daddy.

My mommy is very beautiful. She is an artist.

My sister is three. She likes all animals.

On weekends my daddy takes us on long walks to the nearby park. He knows a lot because you have to study for a long time to become a good pilot. I like to listen to his stories about our planet, the sky, and airplanes.

The alley in our park is lined with giant oak trees.
One time I asked Daddy where the trees come from.
Daddy picked up several acorns from the ground under a
tree and showed them to me in his hand.

"Each of these tiny acorns will turn into a big oak tree," he explained. I thought he was joking and began to giggle. But Daddy continued seriously, "In order to grow into a large tree, the seed must be exposed to sunlight."

"Sunlight?" I asked and looked up at the sky.
Daddy pointed to the leaves on the tree, "All
green leaves have a magical juice inside them."

"Magical?" I asked. "I love magic! Our teacher at school,
Miss Joy, showed us magic tricks. They were a lot of fun."

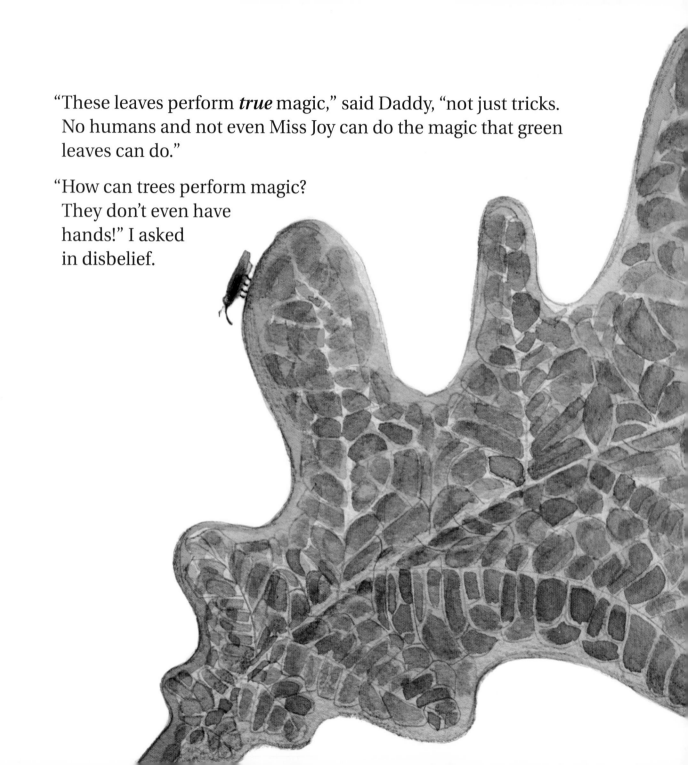

"These leaves perform *true* magic," said Daddy, "not just tricks. No humans and not even Miss Joy can do the magic that green leaves can do."

"How can trees perform magic? They don't even have hands!" I asked in disbelief.

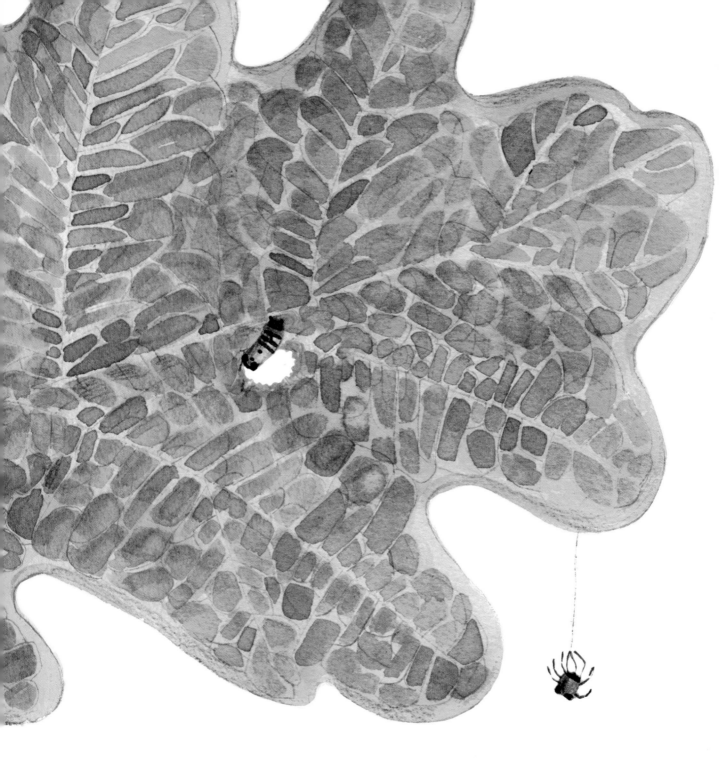

"Plants produce a special green juice from sunlight," said
  Daddy, "This wonderful juice is called chlo-ro-phyll."

"Sunlight may seem to be invisible and not important.
  However, plants can turn it into a green juice that
  we can see and touch."

"Plants build their leaves, branches,
    bark, roots, and even trunks
    from that green juice."

Chlorophyll

"Bark from juice?"
I asked in amazement.

Daddy approached a very tall tree and tried to shake it. The branches of the tree moved just a little even though Daddy was so strong. I also tried to shake the tree, but it didn't move at all.

"We can say that the trunk of this oak is made out of sunlight, and that, I think, is pure magic," said Daddy.

I put an acorn in my pocket. "I will show it to Miss Joy at school tomorrow. Maybe we can grow an oak tree in our classroom."

"It takes many years for the trees to grow that big," continued Daddy,
"But look at the grass near the sidewalk. It grows up to our knees in
just one summer. Without sunlight the grass also wouldn't grow."

I thought for a few minutes, and then asked, "When we went to the beach in the summer, there were many people lying in the sun; did they all want to grow taller?"

Daddy smiled. "Humans cannot grow from sunlight like plants. Only plants can turn sunlight into magical green juice. People who want to grow taller can eat more green plants, like spinach and lettuce."

"Will I reach the door knocker sooner if I eat more lettuce?" I asked.

"It will definitely help," Daddy replied.

We returned home at dinnertime. "Mommy,
please give me more lettuce," I requested.

"Wow, my healthy boy!" she exclaimed, and she
added a few leaves of lettuce to my dinner plate.

I started to eagerly chew them, and found that I couldn't eat more than one leaf. It was too bitter. I sighed.

"What's wrong, honey?" Mommy asked.

"I want to eat more green leaves so I can grow tall like an oak tree and reach the door knocker, but I cannot eat them all." I sighed again.

Mommy looked thoughtful.

Daddy called Lily and me into the living room to read a book before bed. I joined them but had a hard time listening. I kept thinking about the magic juice, the big trees, and the bitter lettuce.

The next morning on the way to school,
I kept looking at the oak trees in admiration.

In the evening, when I came home from school, I noticed a huge box in the kitchen. "Mommy, what is in the box?" I asked.

"I found a trick to eating a lot of lettuce in a delicious way," she explained.

I became curious.

We opened the box, and found a kitchen appliance inside. "This is our new blender," Mommy said. "Before dinner, we will make a green smoothie."

"What is a green smoothie?" I asked

"Remember the magical green juice that the oaks made out of sunlight?" Daddy asked.

I remembered very well: big trees made out of sunshine.

"So, the green smoothie is a magical juice for humans," Daddy explained.

I became excited. "I want to try it!"

Daddy brought a huge basket of produce into the kitchen. I helped unpack a big yellow mango, a bunch of bananas, a pear, and a whole bag of lettuce.

Mommy washed the lettuce in the sink,
while daddy put the blender together.

Lily and I peeled the bananas.

Then we placed the fruit and the greens into the blender and added some water.

"Cover your ears," Mommy said, "there will be a big noise." The bananas, mango, and lettuce quickly disappeared in the blender. It all turned into a smooth green liquid.

Mommy picked out fancy cups from the cupboard. She poured the green mixture into them.

I remembered the bitter taste of lettuce and was afraid to try the green smoothie. But I was curious and took a sip anyway.

The green smoothie was amazingly sweet!
I drank the whole cup and asked for another.

I looked out of the kitchen window. The branches on the big oak tree were moving in the wind as if they were waving to me. I waved back and showed them my cup of smoothie.

Now I can grow big and strong too.

Nic's Favorite Smoothie

3 cups spinach

2 cups apple juice

1 cup water

1 ripe mango, peeled, seed removed

1 banana, peeled

1 orange peeled, seeds removed

Blend well